AuthorHouse™
1663 Liberty Drive
Bloomington, IN 47403
www.authorhouse.com
Phone: 1 (800) 839-8640

Published by AuthorHouse 07/16/2019

ISBN: 978-1-5246-7319-2 (sc)
978-1-5246-9122-6 (hc)
978-1-5246-7320-8 (e)

Library of Congress Control Number: 2017906947

Print information available on the last page.

authorHOUSE®

Splotches

Janet Gomes

My name is Splotches.
I am a male cat.

When I was a baby cat I did not
have a nice home. I was very sad.

But some nice ladies found
me and took care of me
at Petsmart shelter.

Now I am 2 years old and waiting for someone to adopt me.

One hot summer day, a family came to Petsmart to adopt a dog. But Petsmart didn't have any dogs that day. However, they had lots of cats for adoption.

My new mommy pet me
for a longtime.

Her parents said agreed to
letting her adopt me.

Now I have a new home.

My new family loves me so much and takes care of me.

I get to eat my breakfast before anyone else in the house. I love to eat.

They feed me my favorite foods. When I am good I even get yummy treats.

I never like to take bath.
I try to cry like a baby.

They clean me and give me
baths when my paws get dirty.

I look very gorgeous
after taking bath.

I even get extra hug from
everyone in the house.

Everybody loves to pet me,
especially my new mom.

She likes to carry me and
cuddle me all the time. She
even made me a sweater.

I love to sleep on her bed.

I have my own bed. But it's not as comfy as my mom's bed.

Sometimes, I take more space for me.

My mom doesn't mind at all. She really loves me dearly.

Now in my new home, I can
bathe in the sun light.

I can take long naps
in cozy places.

I am a very well behaved cat. I can sit when they ask me to.

I do not rip anything in the house.

I am always with someone in the house. I don't like to be alone.

They all know me very well.

I know cool tricks like
how to jump in the air.

I have so many toys to play with.

One of the toy is a bouncy
ball. I use my front paws
to throw it in the air.

Then I jump high to catch it.
Everyone likes to watch me.

One day, I threw a ball from second floor and it landed inside the standing lamp.

I ran to catch it and and I ended up hanging from the standing lamp.

Then, I fell on the floor with the standing lamp. I broke the lamp.

But, no one got mad at me.

I try not to do that again.

I can play with cool toys whenever I want.

I like to jump up high on the air and chase feathers.

And the best part of my new
home is that everybody loves me!

~inted in the United States
kmasters